Dreams Have a Meaning

OF LOVE AND DEVOTION

Bill Richardson

Intertype
Melbourne, Victoria

Bill Richardson C/- Intertype Publish and Print
Unit 45, 125 Highbury Road
BURWOOD VIC 3125
Australia
www.intertype.com.au

Ordering Information:
Quantity sales. Special discounts are available on quantity purchases by corporations, associations, and others. For details, contact the "Special Sales Department" at the address above.

Dreams Have a Meaning/ Bill Richardson. —1st ed.
ISBN 978-0-6453780-5-4

Contents

Introduction

Whilst reading these verses I hope, you like I will let your mind re-live those days of old, when you believed in fantasy from which you derived so much happiness. Also, to relate to nature to embrace the beauty we derive from her surroundings. Accepting mankind had no input into that which nature has endowered us there is one verse, to which I compare mankind to the changing seasons. The personal verses relate to those of us who suffered the loss of a loved one.

A Rain Drop Fell

Life first began when a rain drop fell
to form a pool, in a faraway dell
that pool soon grew, then began to flow
giving life to all, the land below

That pool became, a running steam
leaving life where, it had never been
over rocks, through valleys, it forged ahead
in time, to form a riverbed

Now fish can breed, where this river flows
and along its banks a forest grows
within this forest, birds now nest
and wild life, find their place to rest

Each sound they make, would seem to be
sweet music, sung in harmony
which carry through, to openings clear
to drift on by, for us to hear

"These things" took place, not because of man
"a rain drop fell, then life began"

Maurine's Last Battle

My time has come, I'm frail and weak
this pain won't stop, to let me sleep
just let it be , what is to come
I've fought a battle, that can't be won

I know your sad, that you feel for me
but understand this has to be
its "now" this day, more than all the rest
your love for me, must stand its test

We've had our trials, over many years
But still your here, to wipe my tears
for my time has come, of that we know
please hold my hand, and let me go

For the where I go, all pains end
please stay with me, until the end
just hold me close, and smile for me
it will be the last, my eyes will see

We shared so much, throughout the years
such love, such joy, and sometimes tears
but the time has come to say, "goodbye"
it's time to close my eyes, and?

Reaching Out

I write this note, not knowing your name
in hope these words, are not in vain
I feel for you, having lost your pride
like feeling empty, being cast aside

A feeling you get, when without a friend
we've all had that feeling, "it isn't the end"
harsh words maybe said, but this I say
you're in control, just turn walk away

Yes, turn the next corner, go down a new street
for you never know, just who you may meet
it maybe "me", or someone else who
has hoped all their life, they'll get to know you

Please go live your life, and maybe someday
we'll get to meet, if you pass my way
my doors always open, your welcome inside
so come on in, I've nothing to hide

I'm hoping to meet you, for when I do
I know that our meeting, will help me "too"
many folks out here, lend a helping hand
but they need "your" help, to understand

A Life Begotten

There cometh the dawn, the sun does rise
its golden rays, engulfing skies
below the earth, doth now awaken
to natures gifts, there for taking

In forests, birds, now part their nest
Below a pheasant, with its golden crest
flora awakens to welcome bees
tilting side to side, in a gentle breeze

Thou, now awakes, and begin to sigh
from the nursery, hear your baby cry
thou cradle it, close to thy breast
feeling comfort now, your baby rests

These joys above, don't take for granted
cherish this life a life enchanted
lest within thy heart, be it not forgotten
the wonderous joys, your life's begotten

Sent From Heaven

An angel came from heaven, to spend a life on earth
The purpose of your coming, was to be here for my birth.

You were the perfect angel, he sent from up above
To nurture to take care of me, to smother me with love.

You were also here to guide me, to teach me right from wrong
You showed me how to cope with life, the way to get along.

Life wasn't always easy, and when trouble came my way
I always found my comfort, in words that you would say

All the things you taught me, still are part of all my days
To love, to show compassion, they help in many ways

Now time has passed, and so have you, your back there up above
Though I'm still here, I'm not alone, I'll always have your love

I'll cherish all the memories, of the life we shared together
Can't say how much, you meant to me, forget you, never ever

I loved you more than words could say, could never be another
It made me proud I had the love, of the world's greatest "mother"

My Daughter

The Day I had to stop and think, of a new girl in my life
Was the day when I was given, "a daughter", by my wife

A child so sweet, can't touch her yet, so tiny so petite
But already she is in my heart, which I feel, has another beat

We bought you home, you'd start to crawl, then begin to walk
I'm so amazed times gone so fast, for now you start to talk

Then when we'd shop, could not resist, those eyes like skies of blue
We'd buy so much, but still you'd beg, I, buy the bride doll too

Don't worry bout a son they say, he'll find a new girl every day that,
But "she's" only sixteen, never been kissed, don't kid yourself they say

And then one day, she bought him home, bringing fears I'd always felt
My thoughts were all of saying "no" then like ice, I'd start to melt

She soon became the woman, of whom I am so proud
She chose the man she would marry, to her wishes I had bowed

Nothing more to teach her, as she goes upon her way
So, I hope and pray this love I have, lives in her heart each day

The Things We Did

Those early days, when first we met
the walks we'd take, even in the wet

We'd learn the lyrics, of the latest song
to sing together, as we ambled on

Those times were fun, but now somehow
it's true, we can never, do them now

So often we danced, till the early morn
not getting home, till the break of dawn

To the parks we'd go, glide on swing
admiring the beauty, of birds on wing

Now times passed by, and like before
those things we never, do anymore

The years have passed, and now your life
I was so proud my darling, you were my wife

My memories of you, will live forever
forget you not, "no" never ever

I'll dream instead, and this I vow
one day my darling, to find you, somehow

Peace Of Mind

You're awakening now, to start a new day
soon to be ready, to go on your way
Time to think what's, ahead for you
there are so many things, in life you can do
Like those visit those thoughts that exist in your mind
you can travel that journey, to seek and find

Why not go sail away, to visit all lands
see all the beauty, mother nature commands
Like trees in the forests, where birds can rest
and then in the spring build their nests
Or follow those rivers, that flow to the coast
were oceans wait them, to act as their host

Climb those mountains, that reach for the sky
or just sit and gaze, at the/world passing by
Go see a volcano, a spectacular sight
try catching-a star, oh what a delight
You could go fly a kite, in meadows so green
but whatever you do, go follow your dream

We're given the choice, to choose what we do
so, think very carefully, of what's best for you
Don't chase all those hopes, to gain fame or wealth
instead concentrate, on what's best for your health
Only then will you know, your life's been defined
you'll know in your heart, you've found peace of mind

Equality

By day the farmer sows his field, at evening, tends his cow
Our lives, are not so different, we're all the same somehow

We live our lives most every day, passing people on the street
Not thinking of, lives they lead, is that wary/ being discreet

Our lives are often filled with joy, there can also be a tear
We live with hope, heartaches too, we can also live-in fear

Often, we will face a storm, or bask beneath the sun
Sometimes suffer biting pain, other times life's, full of fun

So, as you face, your life each day, please think what you can do
try to give a helping hand to others just like you

So, face the fact, we're not so different to others that we meet
Life doesn't choose, who gets to share, the bitter or the sweet

A Night In My Life

It's evening time, time for bed, time for me to sleep
I close my eyes, mum tucks me in, I'm trying not to peek
She kisses me "Pooh Bear" too, and lays him by my side
Her tender tones, her gentle touch, fill my heart, with pride

She's reading me, a nursery rhyme, bout a woman in a shoe
Who has a son, "what's" his name? Oh, they call him little boy blue
And there's his friend, with whom he spends most days
He's in a corner, his names "Jack Horner" it's kinda where he stays

There's also a kid called "little Tom Thumb" he's very hard to find
He's not very big "I'm" bigger than him, they say, he's one of a kind
Been a long night, not over yet still looking for, a friend I met
His name is thumper, he's rabbit, and I'd love him for my pet

Now I'm awake, I'll tell my mum, about my newfound friends
 if she agrees, I'll invite them round, but on her, it all depends
So, when you sleep, go visit this place, its full of so much glory
Can't say much more, it'd take too long, it's a never-ending story

Love And Devotion

That, love, and devotion, both, full of emotion
unconditional, that's as deep, as the ocean
there, to guide, many, lost without sight
to clear their way, and lesson their plight

At morn when you awake, they'll be there at your feet
awaiting your rise, they, then you to greet
there protect you, by day or by night
an embrace, you may give, they accept with delight

When toddlers annoy, as they do each day
they just wag their tails, saying, that's okay
the love they bring, could never measured
let's hope, that love, will always se treasured

As you lay to rest please, recall, what's begotten
that love, so faithful, let be not forgotten
if that love they gave, meant, so much to you
it's your turn, to give to them, what they given you

A Dream Come True

The day has come your born a son, your dream at last come true
Your feelings you can't hold within, of what he, means to you
And now he's yours, there is the need, to find this boy a name
While doing so, also plan, his future, and his fame

Turned one, then two, three, and four, and now he's turning five
He's running wild, he never stops, what gives this boy his drive
Loves to shop, with roving eyes, to see just what he'd like
A train, a plane, a cricket bat, "oh"- he's settled, for that bike

Didn't seem so long, but came the day, many things he's packed away
Things with which he often played, in his mind they'll always stay
He's changed, he's grown, you've done all you can
You've watched with pride, and before your eyes, he's become a man

And now, as he makes his way through life
Will he next desire, be to take a wife
For when he does, let's hope and pray
His wife will bear, his son one day

True Love

A star fell from heaven, bringing truelove my way
Transforming my life, on that wonderful day

With your, soft blue eyes you looked toward me
Smiling, so beguiling, as a woman can be

I knew in my heart, my life it had changed
You'd come from heaven, as if pre-arranged

Fifty years have passed, since we both took our vows
Those memories, so many, to cherish are ours

We loved, we honoured, for better, or worse
Even during the times, things became terse

Now you have left, for a place far away
I'll miss you darling, but this last thing I pray

That you'll wait for me, for my promise to you
is, to join you someday, our love to renew

To My Daughters

A note to tell you, I'm here up above
"me" your mother, my sweet turtle doves

Although you can't see me, believe me, I'm here
I know what you're feeling, your thoughts are so clear

It's there in your hearts, I'll always remain
this I must tell you, I'm now free from pain

Yes, I'm here gazing down, hoping that you
take care of each other, I'm trusting you to

There's much more in life, you must figure out
fulfilling your dream, is what life's about

So don't give up, still follow your dreams
its then you'll know, what happiness means

For finding your dream, brings peace from within
its then you'll find, your life will begin

A Day In My Life

What a day this has been, with my teddy bear, friend
full of fun and excitement, from beginning to end

But now that it's over, and days turned into night
it's time for bed, and to turn out the light

Before I do that, don't let me forget
to give "rags" a cuddle, "rags"? Oh, he's my pet

Mum tries to rush me, saying she's lots to do
I'm sparing for time, un-doing my shoe

I've lined up the kids at the end of my bed
there's batman and robin, pooh bear, and ted

It's, time for a story, so here comes mum
but before the story, we both have some fun

The stories sound good, but I go round the bend
she's such a slow reader, I'm asleep when they end

What's on for tomorrow? I haven't thought yet
but I'll be in more trouble, on that you can bet.

I'm There Close By

Thou cometh to where I lay to rest
among the trees, where birds can nest
but I'm not here, I could not sleep
I'm there with you, as thou doth weep

I'm the sun that shines, across the plain
I'm the gentle touch, of falling rain
a summer wind, that softly blow
I'm there among, the falling snow

I'm the rising moon, that shines so bright
I'm a shining star, thy guide each night
when cometh the dawn, as thou doth wake
'twas I who gave, that gentle shake

so come not, to my grave, to cry
for I'm not here, I'm there close by.

Soul Mate

When'st, thou came to me, as I lay a night
thou filled my heart, with sheer delight
You cared for me, as you saw the signs
of me going through, my darkest times

To have you by, gave me strength indeed
to touch your hand, was all I'd need
Being with you, just to have you there
I'd feel I'd found, a love so rare

Then you bore, our precious child
a gift from heaven, so meek so mild
You looked at me, thy soft lips smiling
your eyes of blue, were so beguiling

Throughout our lives, not all went well
but our love endured, that's all to tell
Then cometh day, you left this life
I'll cherish your memory, my dearest "wife"

Our Vet

Loving, caring, compassionate too
a few words chosen, when describing you

We bring you our "pets", in hope they be cured
after wise words from you, to feel reassured

You treat them with care, devotion, and skill
to see them as we do, while your duty fulfill

As much as we try, it's so hard to begin
to describe that love, you show from within

A beautiful person, you are that's so true
doesn't seem quite enough, just to say we "thank you"

Love

"Love" a phrase, used in many a way
can be used to describe, a lovely day
Or as puppy "love", we had at school
if rejected, how we felt a fool

When young 'twas often, we'd "love" to pray
our wish to came true, most every day
We'd "love" to sing, our favourite song
and to "love" the feeling, we belong

"Love" to run my fingers, through your hair
"love" the way you move, around with flair
To express true "love", to be sure it's heard
your heart must echo, "every word"

Like your baby's "love", can't be denied
when giving birth, with joy, you cried
For that's the "love" I've given you
since the day we, met, since you said "I do"

Changes

Do you ever think, as you go your way
of changes, taking place each day

From a frosty morn, at early light
to a lovely day, as the sun shines bright

As seasons change, as they always do
there's so much more, awaiting you

How tides do change, with the rising moon
how your spirit drops, in an empty room

Your plans can change, it's also true
come a summer storm, out of the blue

So please be careful, in all you do
lest people, see a change in you.

Let's Walk

Come with me, walk this forest trail
enjoy the aroma, there to inhale
It comes from trees, bending in the breeze
swinging back and forth, with so much ease

In autumn as, their leaves do fall
they cover this trail, just like a shawl
A flock of birds go flying by
adding beauty, to a clear blue sky

Beside this trail, there's a running stream
leaving life, wherever it has been
There is so much flora, it's all around
where wildlife roam, hard to be found

As we walk this trail, always winding
we add to the joys, were always finding
like flora, inter-twinning trees
fed with pollen, spread by the bees

At evening time, the forest rests
and birds return, back to their nests
These forests and fauna, were all god's plan
he made them before, "creating man"

Friendship

Throughout our lives, we find many a friend
most friendships last, then, some may end
It's not because, you've grown apart
often, they seek a brand-new start

We wish them well, in their new endeavour
but forget them no, no never ever
For they like family, were there all through
always helping, and supporting you

We must be strong, hold back that tear
there on their way, that's oh so clear
Their cherished memories, are yours to keep
retain that thought, do not weep

Though life disappoints, we all must cope
for life can also, give us hope
You never know, may come the day
when your life beckons, "you" on your way

Maurine's View Of Heaven

I'm sending this note, to say what goes' up here
there's no more worries, there's nothing to fear

There is no time, there are no clocks
no doors to close, there are no locks
There are no races, no colours or creeds
no anger, no fights, no evil deeds

When you arrive, no bells to be ringing
you know you're there, you hear angels singing
You gain entry through, the pearly gate
no need to hurry, there's no long wait

"Saint Michael's" there, to welcome you
with outstretch wings, saying come on through
Now once inside, you'll not impose
for after all, it was you "he" chose

Your now in "heaven", or to be precise
it's also known as "paradise

Footnote:

While reading her view of heaven, I notice Maurine makes no mention of wine bars, happy hours or finding a prospective drinking partner. Somehow I don't think this will be to her liking. I won't be surprised to that she has broken curfew and goes down below to that other place to see if they have anything to offer,

Eighteen

Spring brings beauty, to this land of ours
our trees are with blossom, upon their boughs

Flowers though meadows, what a wonderful scene
hillsides are covered, in carpets of green

Yet a greater wonder, has come to life
a child is born, to a husband and wife

She's a bundle of joy whom they name "Michelle"
her beauty is such, many words oh to tell

From a baby to a child, now a "woman" today
her parents so breathless, no words to say

Soon she'll leave, many lands she will roam
to conquer life's mysteries, now on her own

Childhood Dreams

it's time for bed, so I'll say goodnight
had a lovely day, filled with delight

Won't be long I'll be dreaming, as I often do
you're welcome to join me; I hope that you do

On a magic carpet, we'll fly through the sky
seeing thing's dreams are made of, go passing by

We begin our journey, in the enchanted land
we can venture together, as you're holding my hand

Up here you'll meet peter, and captain hook too
behind them, there's a woman, who lives in a shoe

Quick, look over there, gee, that's tinker bell
I felt she was near, when that star dust fell

Come let's climb up there, to the top of that hill
I believe those two kids, are jack and jill

And who's that sitting on top of that wall
why, it's Humpty, who's trying so hard not to fall

Keep walking my friend, for the further we go
I hope to see Santa, ride off through the snow

Before this dream ends, look for snow white and cinder
two girls that I knew from a book back in kinder

Gee, I'm starting to waken, so it must be morning
I can tell cause I lay here, stretching and yawning

Now I'm rubbing my eyes, cause the sandman has been
he always comes, when I'm havin' a dream

Let's hope someday, we can meet once again
for another journey, down memory lane

For now, save your dreams whatever you do
remember my friend, " dreams can come true"

Old Friends

Do you recall your, friends of old
around the time, being two years old
Great to know, were so much fun
I'm sure, I met mine, through my mum

Like haunting song, from yester year
do you get that feeling, there still here
Most lived-in boxes, under my bed
some in, pop up books, I often read

Those times were great, when it all begun
although we've aged, they still look young
I'm, bowing out, don't get me wrong
but our children's worlds where they belong

Now seems the time, to say goodbye
don't ask my reason, I don't know why
Cep't to say, it's sad but true
I feel it's the best thing, that I should do

The Comparison Of Life To The 4 Seasons

1st there is the spring, the beginning of all new life, when nature transforms our landscapes into a sea of bursting colour and growth, the blossoms, the lilies the vast hillsides carpeted with green so much beauty for us to behold, though so much beauty surrounds us, is there none more breathtaking than when in the spring of our lives, nothing can compare with greatest gift of all, is there anything more beautiful than the sparkling eyes of a new born child, truly the greatest of gifts nature gives to us.

2nd comes the summer of life, a time of fulfillment, the seeds the crops the trees have all grown. Their fruits have ripened their seeds are spreading, carried by the winds to their new pastures, and just like the birds, our children "now teenagers" in the season of youth, are leaving their nests starting to wander, leaving the umbrella of care ,they like the daffodils, must now stand strong against the winds and storms that nature sends their way they too find new roots and they becomes hard to see , for like a rose, they will become hidden in the multitude of thorns, they will learn of infinite things "socializing" becoming impatient, sure they will retain much of what they learn but, just like the flowers, the birds and the bees, only memories will tell their story

3rd the autumn of life is a time of so many changes , in spring new life was beginning, summer we'd harvest all we could, but now, leaves have turned brown, and soon will fall, and like the birds who flew south to build their nests, to raise families of their own, our children now adults, will do the same, and just as the trees have shed their leaves we must do the same it's time for to let them go, it is now their turn to bear fruit

4th finally comes winter, which to me replicates old age, for just as nature's landscape has changed. Over time, we also have changed, for we, no longer full of life, are just like the trees that have shed their, leaves' and are no longer baring fruit, we/they, stand bare and frail, some to wither away some may have the strength to continue for a few more seasons, till nature says, "it's time", it's then, as nature's landscape, continues to evolve, not even a shadow will be seen to tell of our /their existence

This Guy

Do the words I write,-within each poem
seem from some guy, you've never known
Each word I write, comes from my heart
but from my lips, could never part

My life was ruled, by low esteem
which made it hard,-to chase my dream
The only words, I spoke out loud
was on that day, I felt so proud

So, with these words, of love for her
it's plain to see, of how things were
To have loved her, in so many ways
I'll cherish that, throughout my days

These words, from a man, who adored his wife
explain this stranger, who shared your life
This love expressed, so very true
here, my darling "I give to you"

Together Again

these words I write, there not in vain
I know someday we'll meet again

I'll reach to touch your finger tips
then kiss the softness of your lips

the love we had I knew was true
as are the memories I hold of you

As I lay at night, my heart in pain
can't count the times, I call your name

Your every thought, your every sound
can't face the fact you're not around

Please wait for me it won't be long
till I'm there with you where I belong

Then I'll take your hand and we will be
standing side by side for eternity

Thank You Mum

Our memories, they are meant to stay
to recall again, some future day
The fondest ones, I'll always keep
when at night, you'd lay me down to sleep

I'd make you wait, I was never ready
till I cuddled up, with my friend teddy
You'd tuck us in, then we would fly
on a magic carpet, through the sky

My mind would race as it all began
Then I meet a friend, called "Peter Pan"
And while we spoke, some star dust fell
Then I met this girl, called Tinker Bell

Then altogether, we'd each hold hands
as we wandered through, enchanted lands
Yes, they were the best of times
when you'd read me, all those nursery rhymes

But as time went by, t'was sad but true
those mystic times, I soon outgrew
Still each story time, bought so much pleasure
those times with you, I'll always treasure

Meant For Each Other

To seek knowledge a wisdom, we go back through the ages
finding quotes and phrases, to fill many pages
Like "beauty personified", so rarely expressed
a phrase which depicts, above all the rest
Of the few so entitled, to dwell in this realm
their to be found at the top of the helm

Though rare to behold, such beauty and charms
I was blessed when they came, to rest in my arms
The look in her eyes, captivating beguiling
rose coloured cheeks, her soft lips smiling
My heart was pounding, 'twas so full of love
an angel from heaven had come from above

Many years passed on by, our lives re-arranged
though my love for her, not once has it changed
The world seemed to love her; she was one of a kind
so friendly to others, she bought peace of mind
On the day you were born, I knew you would love her
you were meant for each other, "you" and your "mother"

These Wonders Of Ours

In these lands of ours, stretching coast to coast
are wonderous scenes, never seen by most

Niagara has, those massive falls
grand canyons with their towering walls

Mighty rivers flow, within our lands
deserts that change, by wind swept sands

Those mountain peaks, all covered in snow
present to us, a wonderous show

Australia's north, with its reef lined coast
a wonder of which, they proudly boast

In their centre there's, that mighty "rock"
changing colour by the hour of the clock

Not one of these wonders, were made by man
They're all a part, of nature's plan

Catching Up

"Hi" my darling my one sweet love
I'm writing from this place above

I miss your smile, your tender touch
I miss the children, "oh" so much

I'm pleased to say, I'm free of pain.
except this heartache, now and again

Wish I were there to see your face
And hold you in a sweet embrace,

Although we'll meet again, someday
I hope for you, it's far away

But when we do, it's sure to be
for the whole of all "eternity"

Me To You

Each word that I write, is full of my love
Which I'm sending to you, on the wings of a dove

I'm up here in heaven, where nothing seems new
A reminder of times, when I held you

For you were my Christmas, my star on the tree
you were life, you were joy, you were all things to me

'Twas easy to see, through each of your schemes
Just being with you fulfilled all my dreams

And though life has changed, and you're feeling so sad
Remember that things won't always be bad

Please live your life, go follow you dream
In time it won't be as, bad as it seem

When

These words I write, are not in vain
For I know someday, we'll meet again

I'll reach and touch, your finger tips
then feel the softness, of your lips

The love we had was oh so true
like all the memories I hold of you

As I lay at night my heart in pain
can't count the times I call your name

Your every thought your every sound
I treasure that day, when you found

Please wait for me, for it won't be long
till I'm there with you, where I belong

I'll hold your hand, for its meant to be
you and I together for "eternity"

Our Daughter

Like a shining star in the midnight sky
like a will of the whisp she'd pass on by

Her touch like that of a sweet white dove
she's the symbol of eternal love

To see her grow with every day
it wasn't long, she was on her way

'Twas then we hoped that what we taught her
proves helpful to our lovely "daughter"

A Time To Remember

Tell me, what would you give, to have and behold
a treasure more precious, than silver or gold

There is such a gem, given the meek and mild
a gift sent from heaven, for only a child

Why, their given this gift, is so clear to see
it's something that often, eludes you and me

Called "imagination" and so it would seem
it helps them most, when used in a dream

They can travel through space, go swing on a star
carry star dust and moon beams, home in a jar

They can slide down a rainbow, or ride on a broom
but they'll have to hurry, their dreams ending soon

Tell me what you would give, to return to those times
when your life evolved, round nursery rhymes

That time of your life, which gave so much pleasure
when peace of mind, was a thing you would treasure

A Message

A message to my darling daughters "Sue & Jodie"

You may cry many tears-now I'm not there
their only reminders of the love we would share

You'll close your eyes and pray it's not true
for deep in your heart- I've-never left you

Your heart will feel empty-throughout each long day
although I assure you, I'm not far away

You still have your memories-so there's nothing to fear
I've left you enough- for each falling tear

Seems life's not worth living but that won't last long
for then you'll find courage-to fight and go on.

"Mum"

Wish On A Star

It's evening now, been a busy day
I'll say my prayers, then be on my way

If you'd like to come, your welcome too
You're sure to enjoy it, there's lots to do

Our journey starts, aboard "Thomas the Train"
to start' an adventure, down memory lane

First stop we make, is "the enchanted land"
to the wonderous sound, of a marching band

We meet Alice, White Rabbit, the Mad Hatter too
then Tweedle Dee and Dum, will welcome you

We'll continue our journey, going high in the sky
to a land full of memories, of times long gone by

We go over the rainbow, it's a must because
it's the way we gain entry, to the land of "oz"

In there you meet straw man, and the tin man too
and a cowardly lion, who'll try to scare you

Also "Toto"- the "Muchkins" who'll fall at your feet
and a witch from the north, who isn't so sweet

By now the days ending, so it's time we must go
let's slide down the rainbow, to our homes far below

Our journey to dreamland has come to an end
and my homes quite near, it's just round that bend

All those friends we just met, will live in our dreams
their up there on high on distant moonbeams

So, if ever your lonely, or have nothing to do
just wish on a star, they'll come visit you

A Note From Above

To the family I loved, I'm here up above
here with your "mother" my one true love

Although you don't see us, believe me, we're here
we know what you're feeling, your thoughts are so clear

Yes, I'm here holding mum, in my arms once again
Happy to say, she's now free of pain

We're gazing down, watching over you
still feeling proud of all that you do

You've so much in life, to still figure out
such as the hopes, you're always dreaming about

So please don't give, up, go follow your dreams
to find true love, and what happiness means

Once you've found with all it can bring
it then you will find, your life will begin

Nature's Gifts

As the evening sun turns, skies to gold
what a breath-taking sight, mother nature unfolds
The northern skies, with their dancing lights
like shooting stars, in the heavens at night

Volcanos erupting, with fire emerging
strong winds that accompany, seas when surging
The poles, the icebergs, with nowhere to go
peaks of mountains, all covered with snow

Across each meadow, lay carpets of green
flower covered hillsides, in colours serene
Throughout the lands, many rivers unwind
on which we do travel, our future to find

But it's not only visions, mother nature contains
there are sounds of the forests, a bird's sweet refrain
So sadly accepted, taken for granted
these pleasures we note, from land's so enchanted

Though nature provided, these lands so pristine
it's we, get to treasure, this wonderful scene
Though nature it's true, has given so much
it's we who'll give life, it's final touch

For all of this wonder, could never outshine
the beauty possessed by this woman of mine
Not defined by her looks but beauty within
to tell of it all, I'll not try to begin

Cep't her touch, her smile, had what nature contained
they began our journey, and true love has remained
Though natures gifts, may be counted in hours
like eternity endures, will this love of ours.

A Message From "Tiffany"

'Twas a summers day, when first we me
I reached in your heart, and became your pet
Those early days were crazy I know
I'd follow you round, wherever you'd go

To the bedroom, the shower, the lounge didn't care
loved to jump up beside you, on a kitchen chair
Had so much fun, playing ball outside
but come time for a bath, I'd run and hide

As years passed on by, we both showed our ages
and the book of our lives, soon became short of pages
Although growing older, our love just grew stronger
if time would stand still, it could last so much longer

Now my bones are all aching, and I'm feeling the pain
going back to the "vets" becoming in vain
My bodies so frail, can no longer cope
I've tried so hard, not to give up hope

Now's come the day, I can fight no more
as hard as I've tried, I've lost this war
As I'm leaving you now, to find peace up above
I leave you those memories, of my devotion and love

Mummy, It's Me

Your hearts been praying, to find true love
that one day someone, would come from above

There's no need to wait, he's been there a while
he already loves you, especially your smile

You feel life's changed, things, aren't the same
but, he's standing beside you, calling your name

You stand there you wonder, who can this guy be
when a small voice beside you whispers, "Mummy it's me"

A Summer Breeze

It drifted in, on a summer's breeze
like music lilting, through the trees

I knew it not, a chance to miss
to let it pass, would be amiss

How could this be, words questioned me
then beckoned her, to come to me

I reached for her, she took a pace
we stood together, in a sweet embrace

We woke next morn, both of the view
true love had come from out of the blue

Though times gone by, since she passed away
that love we found, still here to stay

Each evening now, I'm among those trees
living memories, of that summer breeze

Style And Grace

Those looks, so cute, your smiling face
were natures gifts, plus style and grace

Your eyes, would brighten up a room
like skies at night, as doth the moon

These words here said, yes are true
though an "angel", more befitting you

Not words well chosen, persuaded me
'twas your sweetness, that attracted me

To describe my feelings, can't begin
c'ept, I believe true beauty lies within

Your every word, your gentle touch
your charming ways, they meant so much

that day you left, there were no goodbyes,
though tears were falling, from my eyes

Even though you've gone, we're not apart
for I hold you here, within my heart

Best Of Dreams

Do you recall the beginning, when you started to dream
you could do anything, or so it would seem

Like go on a journey, fly through the sky
catching star dust and moonbeams, drifting on by

You would travel the world, at the speed of a rocket
catch falling stars, to put in your pocket

Then slide down a rainbow, finding pots of gold
filling your mind, with dreams, still untold

You'd wake up next morn, of a new day begun
raring to tell, of all you had done

Then after that day, you'd return to your dreams
to start new adventures, full-filling your schemes

Now during each day, we can daydream too
but during those dreams, there's a lot you can't do

Yes, the best time to dreams when you've fallen asleep
for they are the dreams you'll want to keep

The Spirit Of Xmas

T'was the night before Xmas, mums lighting the tree it's abounding with presents, what a sight to see

The kids are peeking, guessing what Santa's bought Aaliyah, stands guard-don't want to be caught

Now dad's sneaks a peek, just to be in the fun oh mummies behind him, too late, he's been sprung

It's now Xmas morn, and everyone has arrived tis amazing how quick, this house came alive

There's, grandma & grandpa wiping his tears for he used, to play "Santa" for many long years

Summer is anxious, she's been restless all night that look on face is of sheer delight,

Aaliyah's getting worried, yells some are for "meee"

Now, not every gift, can be bought in a store there are many been shared time & time before

Gifts like "joy" "happiness", and a thing called "love" "compassion" "forgiveness" that come from above

So, let's think of others, and show that we care

Remember them always, when sating a "prayer"

He's Leaving You

This day has come, so sad but true
this man you love, is leaving you
It won't be long, he's no longer there
he'll leave this home, your tender care

There's someone else,- what can you say
She's reason why, he'll leave today
Who is this person, where is she from
without him there, can you hang on

Though he's leaving now that's not to say
this loss you feel, won't go away
They'll never hide, that welcome mat
for you to come, and have a chat

So, on those days, you feel alone
you'll always find that they are home
So come, and meet, their children too
who they'll always, teach, to love you too

As time's gone by, you've always known
that never once, were you alone
For you always knew she was the one
who'd cherish, love, and care, for your son

Dreams

"Dreams" they are wishes that all stem from your heart
a desire built inside you, where all your dreams start

Some wish for treasure, diamonds, or gold
But you'll have to be patient, for your dreams to unfold

Some wish "true love", a rare gift that's true
it's a treasure to cherish, if, that dream comes true

So always be careful, in what you wish for
for if you stop dreaming, there's no chance, anymore

Yes, think what you wish for, is it really your need
maybe wish for another, who needs a good deed

For thinking of others can have its rewards
it can bring peace of mind among other awards

Not only at night, we have all our dreams
there are day dreams too, to hatch many schemes

So, whenever you dream, whenever you start
be certain your dreams, start deep in your heart

Bed Time

When its bed time, mum will sing me a tune
tonight's about, the man in the moon

Who's good friend "twinkles", a little star
I sing to him, the little star, always asking where you are

I know he lives high in the sky, I learned that in a lullaby
so, to reach him guess, we'd have to fly

So, when I sleep, that's what I'll do
and as my friend, your welcome too

We could catch some moonbeams, if you bring a jar
and if your quick, catch a falling star

There'll be lots to do, while we're up there
it's my dream, so who's to care

We could fly all night, there's lots of time
remember, it's "my nursery" rhyme

I've loved this journey, with you my friend
but, when morning comes, this dream will end

Deception

If you search through life, that it may be
to some day find, your wishing tree

And when if found, it would bring your way
joy with riches, a new life to say

Well, if this does, to say come true
then with these things, what would you do

If those new found riches, are just for show
will it change the person, your friends all know

Does vainness rule, your life so much
it causes you, to lose your touch

It would mean you've been deceived
if this is what your mind, believed

ABOUT THE AUTHOR

William (Bill) Richardson, loving Father to 7, Grand Father to 14 and
Great Grand Father to 7 (and counting)
Bill grew up in Melbourne and while, "not the smartest kid on the
block" he went on to become a driver of Melbourne's iconic trams and
latter enjoyed a career as a sales representative.
He discovered travel later in life and quickly developed a keen love of
Asia with over 24 trips so far.
Bill turned to poetry during the COVID lockdowns as a means of
maintaining his "sanity"